PART SIX - UNITED STATES NAVY

By Daniel Madsen

INTRODUCTION

Many ex-sailors interest in the service lives and technical details of their favourite warships often includes a fascination with their demise. Former sailors, whether drafted civilians or careerists, often wonder what became of their old ship. Was she mothballed? Scrapped? Sold to another navy? It was this interest in those old, abandoned ships that resulted in my writing of Forgotten Fleet: The Mothball Navy, and led me to jump at the chance to contribute a volume to Maritime Books' To Sail No More series. Those books are filled with rare photos of Royal Navy vessels as few have seen them, at the end of their days. This volume shows some of the ships of the United States Navy that have outlived their usefulness.

There is something stirring and at the same time melancholy about the rows of abandoned destroyers that once lined the piers at Charleston and San Diego, the acres of empty flight decks that stretched over the water at Boston and Tacoma, the forest of masts that still span the James River and Suisun Bay. These vessels in storage awaited another call to duty. For many ships that call did come. Destroyers paid off at the end of World War 1 were brought back into commission in the tense years preceding America's entry into World War 2. Some were even traded in 1940 to Great Britain in exchange for British bases in the Caribbean. Carriers, battleships, cruisers, destroyers and auxiliary ships of all kind were mobilized for the Korean War. The battleship New Jersey was brought out of reserve for Vietnam, and all four remaining Iowa-class dreadnoughts returned to duty in the final years of the Cold War. Two saw combat a half century after they were laid down and after three decades in mothballs.

Yet the vast majority of warships and auxiliaries were retired without a whisper, and remained in quiet anonymity for five, ten, fifteen years or more. A considerable number were sold to European, Asian or South American navies. Some were sent to the bottom as targets. A few became museum ships. But most of the thousands of ships in the reserve fleet languished in silence as the years rolled by, until the scrapyards took them. Here then is a look at some of the United States Navy ships of the past and present, those that sailed no more.

Daniel Madsen
April 2002

Author's notes:

Daniel Madsen is the author of Forgotten Fleet: The Mothball Navy, and of the upcoming Resurrection: Salvaging the Battle Fleet at Pearl Harbour. He lives in Kenwood, California.

First published in the United Kingdom in 2002 by Maritime Books, Lodge Hill, Liskeard, Cornwall, PL14 4EL

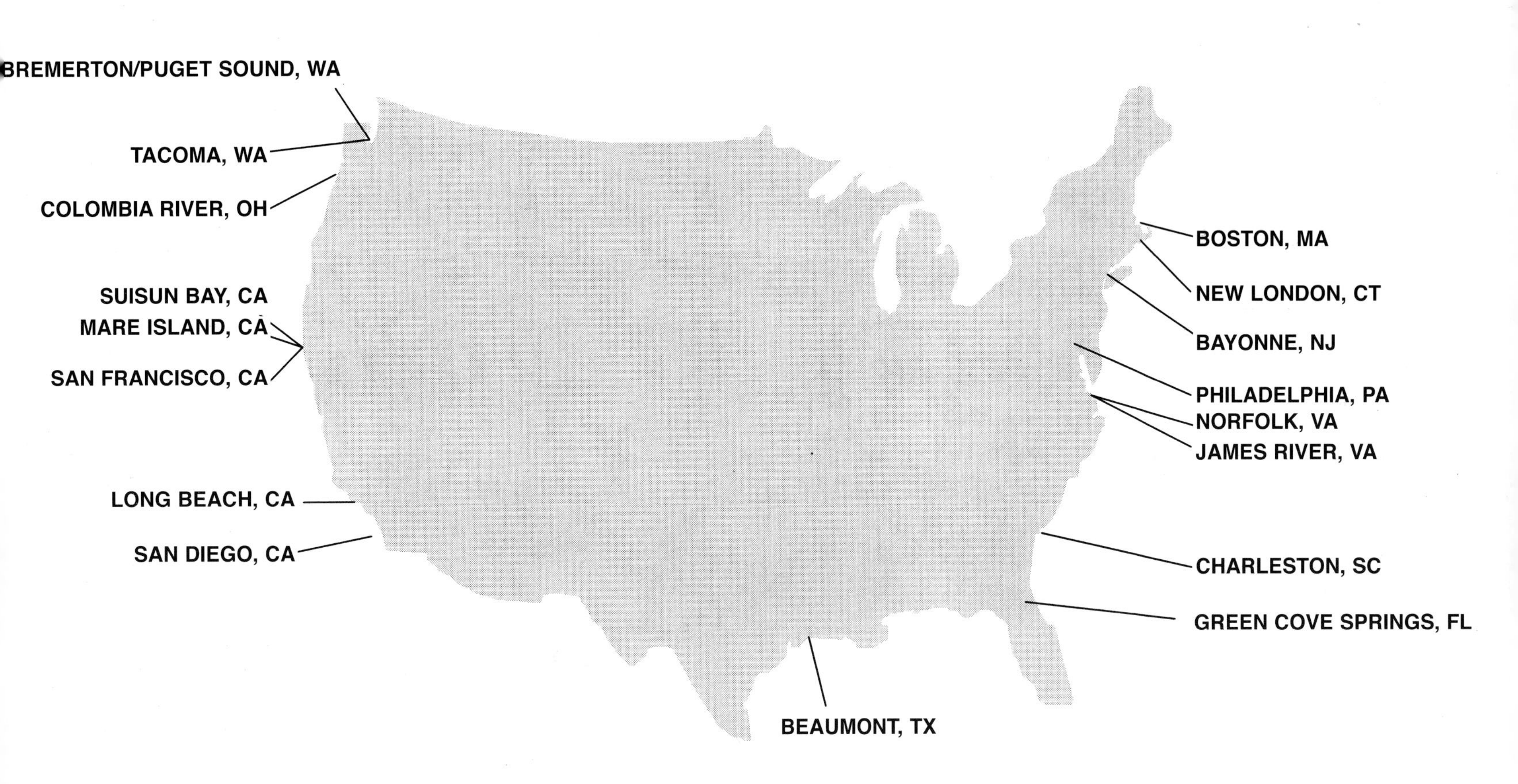

RESERVE FLEET MOORINGS SINCE WORLD WAR TWO

The DELAWARE, commissioned in 1910, was one of 23 battleships, some still under construction, that were scrapped in the early 1920's as a result of the Washington Naval Treaty. The United States, Britain, and other naval powers hoped the treaty would avoid another arms race similar to the one that contributed to World War 1. (Naval Historical Centre)

The mound of big guns from scrapped American battleships is the dramatic and primary result of the Naval Treaty of 1922. Behind the pile the battleship SOUTH CAROLINA is broken up in December 1923. She had been demilitarized, her turrets removed, to be used as a weapons test hulk. Like the DELAWARE she was only 14 years old but already obsolete. (Naval Historical Centre)

Part of the "Red Lead" Fleet at Mare Island on 2 July 1930. The two closest are the flush deck destroyers MERVINE (DD-322) and JOHN FRANCIS BURNES (DD-299). To comply with the restrictions of the London Naval Treaty, both were sold for scrap shortly afterwards.
(National Archives)

The light carrier INDEPENDENCE burns and crackles with radioactivity from the Bikini (Able) atomic test on 1 July 1946. She later survived the second (Baker) test too. With gaping holes in her flight deck she was towed to San Francisco where she remained for more testing until her hulk was sent to the bottom as a target off the California coast in January 1951. (Naval Historical Centre)

The submarines SKIPJACK (left) and SKATE made seventeen war patrols between them. They were then battered, like the INDEPENDENCE, by the pair of Bikini atomic bomb tests in July 1946 that tested the effect of a nuclear blast on naval vessels. Both survived the blasts (the SKIPJACK after being raised from the bottom) and, after being towed back to California for radioactive tests, they were later sunk off the coast.
(National Archives)

This scene of fleet subs and their tender could have been photographed in the South Pacific during World War 2. In actuality it's the quiet waters of San Francisco Bay, and the war has been over for months. These subs had been brought alongside for preliminary work before heading to a yard for a complete overhaul, inventory, and preservation.

(National Archives)

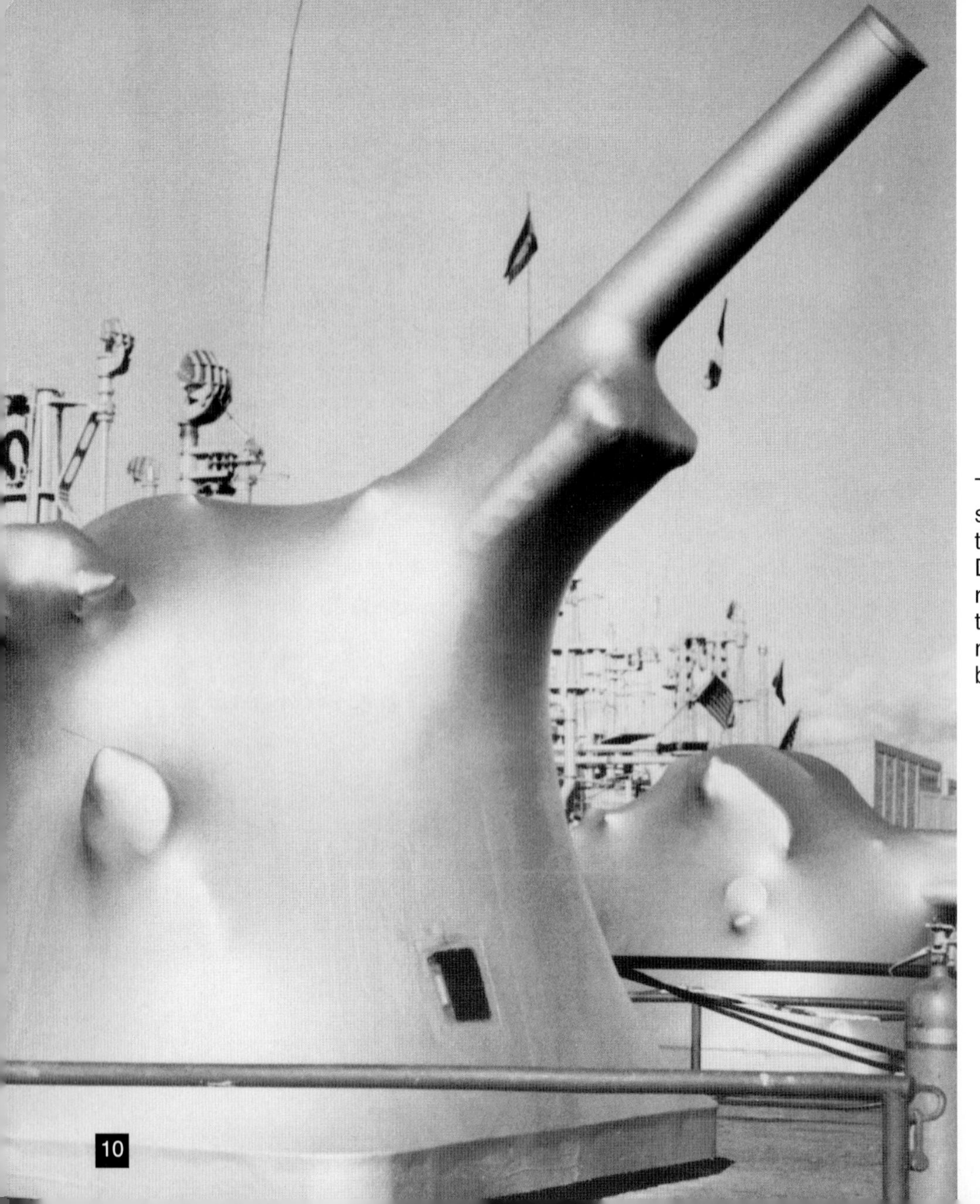

This gun mount was one of thousands upon thousands that were sealed with a rubbery compound that protected the weapon from the elements. Dehumidified air was piped into the mount to retard corrosion. When the ship recommissioned, the film was quickly peeled away. Most such mounts stayed sealed till the ship went to the breakers. (National Archives)

One of the smaller reserve fleet groups was the one at Bayonne, New Jersey, but it contained some of America's best known fighting ships. Seen here in 1953 the ENTERPRISE is at far left. The FRANKLIN is astern, fully repaired after the terrible damage to her in the last year of the war, At the bottom centre of the frame are the battleships NORTH CAROLINA and WASHINGTON. Less well-known are the large cruisers ALASKA and GUAM, forward of the battleships and inboard of an anti-aircraft cruiser. (Battleship North Carolina Museum)

It is 1950, five years after the end of the war, and these escort carriers lie idle at South Boston. Nestled among the “jeep” carriers SUWANNEE and SALERNO BAY is the cruiser DAYTON. None of them ever put to sea again. (Boston Public Library, Print Dept)

Like a ghost ship, the mothballed escort carrier SHIPLEY BAY drifts with the wind and tide some five years after the end of World War 2. She broke loose from her moorings in a storm, the closest she ever came to returning to the sea. (Boston Public Library, Print Dept.)

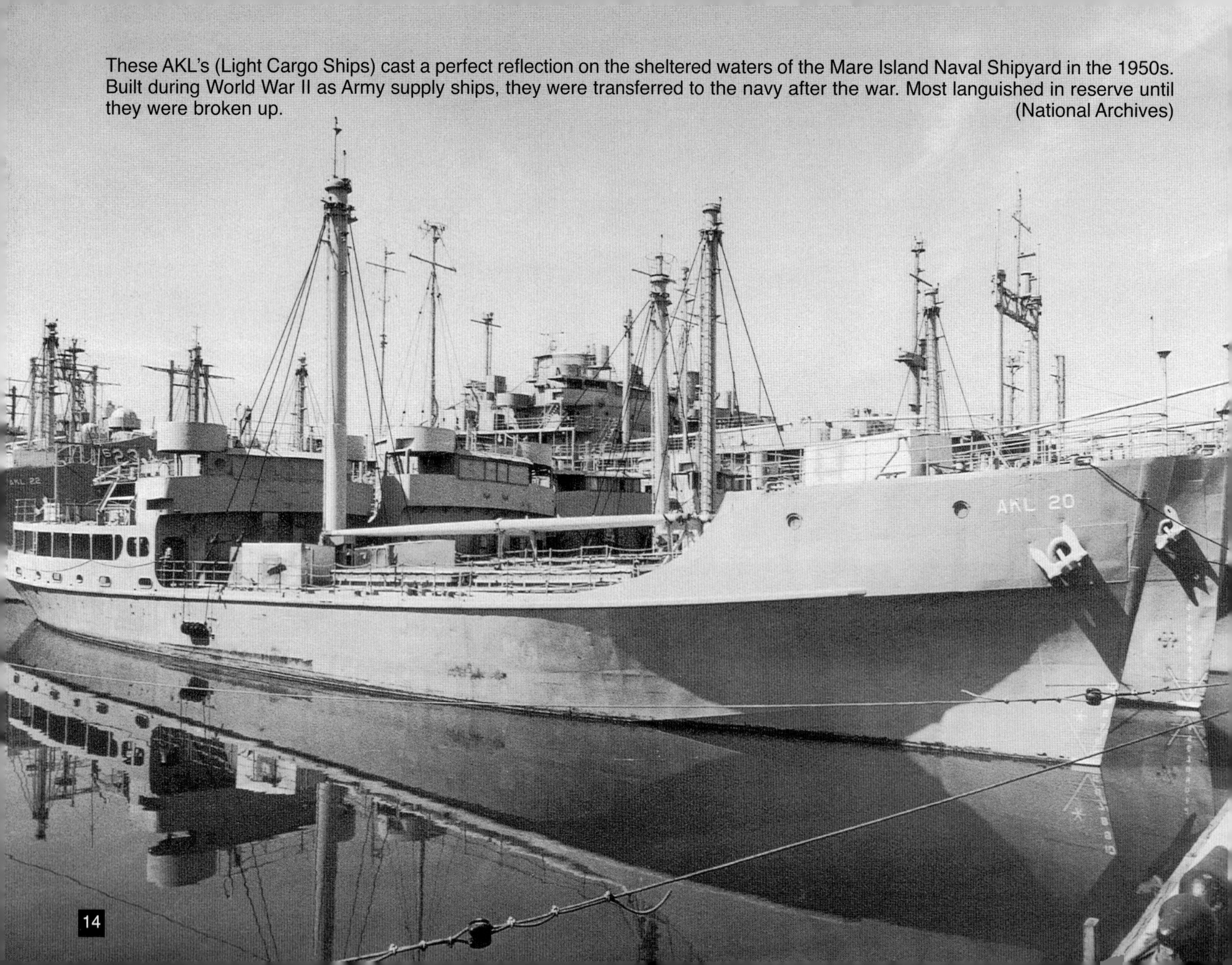

These AKL's (Light Cargo Ships) cast a perfect reflection on the sheltered waters of the Mare Island Naval Shipyard in the 1950s. Built during World War II as Army supply ships, they were transferred to the navy after the war. Most languished in reserve until they were broken up. (National Archives)

The "Big E", the ENTERPRISE, on her way to the breakers on August 11, 1958 after efforts to save this quintessential American warship had failed. The war was long over, the interest in the Navy's most decorated ship had waned. (Joel Shepard)

Although these two rusty ships appear at a glance to be a pair of battleships, a closer look reveals the large cruiser ALASKA tied up outboard of the battleship WASHINGTON. Both were decommissioned in 1947 and went into mothballs at Bayonne; both were stricken in 1960 and were towed here to Kearny, New Jersey to be dismantled. Both had short careers. The WASHINGTON served in the fleet six years, the ALASKA a mere three. (US Naval Institute)

The Oregon City-class heavy cruisers were a modification of the successful Baltimores, but the OREGON CITY herself sailed just 22 months before being laid up for good in December 1947. To the reserve fleet mooring at Philadelphia she went, there to remain, silent and abandoned, while nearly a quarter century passed. The scrap yards at Kearny tore into this nearly unused ship in the mid 1970's as she lay beside the carrier WASP. (US Naval Institute)

Had she been completed, the Iowa-class battleship KENTUCKY might still be on the Navy list in 2001. As it turned out her engines went to the fast combat stores ships SACRAMENTO and CAMDEN, her bow went to replace the damaged WISCONSIN, and the rest of the KENTUCKY, abandoned since work halted on her in 1947, went for scrap. She was towed to Boston Metals in Baltimore in October 1958.
(Naval Historical Centre)

A pair of light cruisers, the Fargo class HUNTINGTON and the Cleveland class DAYTON, and the battleship SOUTH DAKOTA, lie moored together in silence on the Delaware River at the Philadelphia Naval Shipyard in the summer of 1961. The days of all three were numbered and within a year all would be gone from the Navy list. The SOUTH DAKOTA was a scarred veteran of World War II; neither of the cruisers saw more than a few years of peacetime duty with the fleet. (Naval Historical Centre)

This is the hunter-killer submarine BONITA and the odd structure at her bow houses a powerful sonar. She began life as simply the "K-3", one of three submarines built in the early 1950s specifically to track down and sink Soviet submarines. The BONITA and her sisters proved inadequate for the job however and all were decommissioned. (National Archives)

Both of these submarines, the PAMPANITO (SS-383), and BOWFIN (SS-287), escaped the scrapper's torch and became museums. The PAMPANITO went to Fisherman's Wharf at San Francisco and the BOWFIN to Hawaii. Behind them is the sub tender PELIAS, a veteran of the attack on Pearl Harbour on December 7, 1941. (National Archives)

The Korean War had been raging for three months when this photo was taken of the submarine piers at Mare Island in September 1950, but none of these ex-World War 2 boats had been called back to duty. From left DRAGONET (SS-293), MENHADEN (SS-377), MAPIRO (SS-376), SEAHORSE (SS-304), SAND LANCE (SS-381), BATFISH (SS-310), CAPITANE (SS-336), PIPEFISH (SS-388) and LIONFISH (SS-298). (National Archive)

Full House! ...Light carriers, escort carriers, light cruisers and attack transports make up most of the San Francisco Group of the Pacific Reserve Fleet in the late 1950's. These piers were built at the shipyard in the months following World War 2 as the fleet returned home to be paid off. (National Archives)

This photo was taken 21 years after the end of World War 2. Most of these submarines, destroyers and destroyer escorts were to head for the scrap heap within another half dozen years. Some had been recommissioned for the Korean War and then decommissioned again. (National Archives)

The Buckley class destroyer escort OSMUS (DE-701) and the Fletcher class destroyers BULLARD (DD-660) and STANLY (DD-478) are a few of the identifiable old warriors in mothballs at Mare Island in October 1967. Note the flag on the commissioned submarine PAMPANITO. She was mothballed for 15 years after the war before serving again as a training sub. (National Archives)

The light cruiser MANCHESTER, last of the active Cleveland-class 6-inch gun cruisers, is seen shifting berths a few months after being stricken from the Navy List in 1960. She was soon be towed to the breakers. (National Archives)

These are modified fleet submarines, at Mare Island, all commissioned between 1943 and 1946. All were in reserve or stricken by the time this photo was taken in the early 1970's. From left CUSK (SS-348), ROCK (SS-274), CHIVO (SS-341), SPINAX (SS-489), POMODON (SS-486), MEDREGAL (SS-480) and DIODON (SS-349). The ROCK was a veteran of six war patrols. The POMODON was the first "GUPPY" (Greater Underwater Propulsion) conversion of a fleet boat. (National Archives)

Year after year the number of ships in the reserve fleet dwindled as World War II-era ships grow old and are scrapped. Individuality is lost in the jumble of masts, gun mounts, and fading paint. Yet each vessel had it's own unique story to tell. In the far right row are seven Fletcher-class destroyers berthed in the quiet backwaters of San Francisco Bay. Two more are nestled among the two dozen destroyer escorts in this 1963 aerial view of the Mare Island Group, Pacific Reserve Fleet. (National Archives)

The "Mighty Moo", the light carrier COWPENS (CVL-25). An "igloo" seals her forward 40mm mount from the elements and pipes carry dry air into the mount from the ships main dehumidification system. Similar cocoons ring her flight deck, and the gangway, used only by the occasional visitor from the reserve fleet staff, is at her stern. (National Archives)

From 1942 to 1947 she was in commission as the USS MASSACHUSETTS. From 1947 to 1962 she was simply the MASSACHUSETTS, out of commission, in reserve at the Norfolk Navy Yard. Stricken with the other South Dakotas in 1962, she was the ex-MASSACHUSETTS when this shot was taken in 1963. Fate was kind to the "Mamie", she eventually became a memorial and museum in her home state. (Naval Historical Centre)

A World War 2 veteran goes to the breakers. This is the South Dakota class battleship INDIANA being cut apart in Richmond, California after being towed down the coast from Bremerton. On the day this photo was taken, 22 November 1963, another World War 2 Navy veteran named John F. Kennedy, the 35th President of the United States, was assassinated in Dallas, Texas.
(Naval Historical Centre)

The US Navy's first helicopter carrier was the converted escort carrier THETIS BAY. She was mothballed at Bremerton for 9 years before being converted to carry Marines and their assault helicopters. Her second career lasted another 8 years before she was scrapped at Portsmouth, Virginia in 1966. (Naval Historical Centre)

No voices, no bells, no smoke from stacks. No signs of life in this 1960 photograph taken at San Diego. The crews have long since gone. Only silence along the dock, year after year. In the foreground is the Fletcher class destroyer BENNION (DD-662). She was named after the captain of the battleship WEST VIRGINIA who was killed at Pearl Harbour. Still visible are the D/C racks and enclosures for the 20mm and 40mm anti-aircraft weapons. (Naval Historical Centre)

Time has relentlessly marched past these destroyers and destroyer escorts berthed here at San Diego in 1960. They were still cared for by the sailors of the reserve fleet but the chances of any being recalled to duty were slight. (Naval Historical Centre)

At one time it was planned to overhaul each ship in reserve, like these minecraft and escort carriers at San Diego, once every five years. Budget cuts eliminated that within a decade or so after World War II and the ships were overhauled only when going into storage. By the 1970's even that practice was abandoned and the ships were put away with only minimal preservation work and no final overhaul. (Naval Historical Centre)

The Benson class destroyers, like the LIVERMORE, were too small to be modernized with the weaponry needed to counter the Soviet submarine fleet. So they stayed in mothballs until they were all discarded by the late 1960's and early 1970's still retaining their World War 2 weaponry. The pair of igloo-shaped housings covered two of the ships 40mm anti-aircraft mountings in this 1955 photograph. The LIVERMORE was scrapped in 1961.
(Naval Historical Centre)

More than a quarter century after she was pummeled by two kamikaze hits off Okinawa, on 11 May 1945, the BUNKER HILL spent her last years a few yards away from the mud flats at San Diego, serving as an electronic test ship in 1971. Together with the FRANKLIN, she sustained more critical damage than any other Essex class carrier during World War 2. Aluminum igloos still cover some of her remaining 40mm anti-aircraft mounts that were sealed in 1947. (Naval Historical Centre)

Of the 18 Essex-class carriers mothballed at the end of World War 2, only the BUNKER HILL (seen here) and the FRANKLIN were never recommissioned. She was towed from San Diego to Tacoma, Washington, for breaking up in July 1973, looking outwardly much as she did when placed in mothballs in 1947. (Naval Historical Centre)

Commissioned too late to participate in World War 2, the Cleveland class light cruiser PORTSMOUTH spent four quiet years in the Atlantic Fleet before being mothballed at Philadelphia in 1949. She never again stirred. Stricken from the navy list twenty-one years later she was towed down the Delaware River and up the New Jersey coast to Kearny and was cut apart in 1975.
(Naval Historical Centre)

The ocean escort HAMMERBERG waits for the cranes and hammers to slice her apart at Kearny in 1975. The HAMMERBERG was one of the earliest successors to the mass-produced destroyer escorts mothballed after World War 2. (Naval Historical Centre)

The ESSEX was the lead ship of a class of 24 carriers, many of which served from the 40's and into the 70's. She was scrapped at Union Mineral and Alloy Corporation in Kearny, New Jersey, in 1976. To the left are the remains of the carrier WASP.

(Naval Historical Centre)

For every famous ship there were dozens of unfamiliar ones. These destroyer escorts and their fast transport half-sisters in mothballs at San Diego carried equally unfamiliar names: The GOSSELIN (APD-126) was named after a sailor killed on the battleship ARIZONA at Pearl Harbour; the GANTNER (APD-42) after a sailor killed aboard the NEVADA that same day. Though the ships may sail no more, their names live on forever.
(Naval Historical Centre)

The Cleveland class light cruiser VICKSBURG's story was an all too common one for the post war US Navy. Rushed to completion in wartime the cruiser was soon surplus in peace. Built in twenty months, serving just three years, she was a victim of the fleet reduction that sent thousands of ships to the reserve fleet in the late 1940's, most never to return to sea. (National Archives)

Scaffolding covers the mast of the WORCESTER as she is mothballed in 1958 after only a decade with the fleet. She was the lead ship of a two ship calss of cruisers equipped with rapid firing six-inch guns. Her fresh paint and gleaming hull number will soon begin to fade in the salt air while she lies in storage. Fourteen years later she and her sistership ROANOKE were sold for scrapping.
(National Archives)

One of the few Essex class carriers never converted to another role was the ORISKANY. Most became anti-submarine carriers, helicopter carriers or training carriers, but the ORISKANY remained an attack carrier. Construction was suspended on her in 1947 and she was completed in 1950. Her aircraft flew missions in both the Korean and Vietnam Wars. It was while off Vietnam that she was badly damaged by a hangar deck fire in October 1966. The ORISKANY was stricken in 1989, but lasted into the 21st century after being towed from Mare Island to the reserve fleet at Beaumont, Texas. (Daniel Madsen)

She is abandoned here at Bremerton in the late 1990s, her time come and gone, but the MIDWAY still echoes with the sounds of the 200,000 crewmen who served aboard her during 47 years of service. She underwent many conversions during her long career, including a four year rebuild in San Francisco, 1966 - 1970. For years she was the only US carrier based overseas, at Yokosuka, Japan.
(Wiliam Michael Young)

Stripped of her masts, the helicopter carrier TRIPOLI is moored to the waterfront at the now defunct Mare Island Naval Shipyard, where she was being used as a test hulk by the Army in 1996. The TRIPOLI was one of two US warships to be damaged in the 1991 Gulf War when she struck a mine. Four years later she was decommissioned and stricken. (Daniel Madsen)

These two vessels at Mare Island are the dock landing ships POINT DEFIANCE and THOMASTON, built in the late 1950's, seen here up for sale in the 1990's. They were bought by an Oakland company which later defaulted on the sale, forcing the Navy to repossess them and keep looking for a buyer. They were towed to the Suisun Bay Reserve Fleet, where they remain (2002). (Daniel Madsen)

Two generations of destroyers. On the left is the World War 2 Fletcher-class STODDARD, alongside two larger postwar destroyers RICHARD S. EDWARDS and JOHN PAUL JONES. They were saved from scrap only to be used as targets. All were sent to the bottom north of Hawaii, the STODDARD and EDWARDS in 1997, the JOHN PAUL JONES in 2001. (Daniel Madsen)

With a foggy San Francisco skyline in the background, the destroyer LYNDE McCORMICK is tied up outboard of another Charles F. Adams-class destroyer in October 1996. The hull of the McCORMICK has been painted a bright green. These ships, and others, had been purchased by Consolidated Power and Minerals Corporation and stripped of nearly everything except their boilers, turbines and generators to be used as mobile electric power plants. The experiment with the McCORMICK did not pay off and she was later sent to the bottom as a target vessel. (William Michael Young)

Like the LYNDE McCORMICK, all that was needed above deck on the Brooke class frigates (now power barges) RAMSEY and SCHOFIELD are the stacks, to carry away the exhaust as the turbines generate electricity. Like the McCORMICK, the frigates were later sunk as targets. (Daniel Madsen)

Twilight silhouettes these silent cargo and auxiliary vessels at rest at theSuisun Bay Reserve Fleet. Maintenance personnel watch over them, alert to the danger of fire and flooding, keeping the dehumidifiers going, in case they are ever needed again to transport equipment and supplies to a war zone.
(Daniel Madsen)

A starboard quarter view of the OKLAHOMA CITY shows the big Talos missile radars, one for each of her two launchers. She was converted from a gun cruiser in the late 1950's after 10 years in reserve. She served in her new role for another 19 years before being laid up in 1979. Twenty years later she was destroyed as a target. (Daniel Madsen)

The weather is warm but the iron had grown cold when this photo was taken in September 1996 out in Suisun Bay. The hulk on the left is the cruiser ENGLAND, next to her is the GRIDLEY, the frigate LOCKWOOD, and then, the FOX. Names and hull numbers are gone; these ships no longer have Navy identities. All were stricken in the post Cold War reduction of the US Navy. (Daniel Madsen)

Beyond a sea of marsh grass is part of the Suisun Bay Reserve Fleet photographed in 1996. These are World War 2 Victory ships, mass produced cargo vessels that were the successors to the Liberty ships. Unsung heroes of the war, they delivered vitally needed supplies all over the globe for the Allies. (Daniel Madsen)

A closer look shows just how decrepit the old ships appear in 1996, after so many years in the Reserve Fleet. Three Victory ships have been preserved as museum ships, but the vast majority went for scrap long ago. These will join them when a buyer can be found. (Daniel Madsen)

The rounded bow in the middle belongs to the helicopter carrier OKINAWA. Moored to her starboard side is the oiler ROANOKE, and to port are the transports GENERAL JOHN POPE and GENERAL EDWIN D. PATRICK. All were in the Reserve Fleet at Suisun Bay in 1996. (Daniel Madsen)

The fishing can be good out here among these derelicts in Suisun Bay. Moored in a pair off by themselves, not far from the Benicia Bridge, are the minesweepers EXCEL and CONSTANT. (William Michael Young)

From back to front at these Bremerton piers are the carriers HORNET, ORISKANY, BENNINGTON and BON HOMME RICHARD. All were deleted from the Naval Vessel Register in 1989 with the BENNINGTON later being towed to India to be scrapped. BON HOMME RICHARD went to the breakers too, but the ORISKANY has so far (2002) avoided the torch, and HORNET has become a museum at Alameda, in San Francisco Bay. (Defense Visual Information Centre)

The carrier MIDWAY, commissioned just after the end of World War 2, is towed out of San Diego by the fleet tug NARRAGANSETT on her way to the Bremerton mothball fleet after being decommissioned in 1992. She was maintained in reserve for a few years before being stricken, and a group was hoping to tow her back to San Diego in late 2002 as the centrepiece of a new naval museum.
(Defense Visual Information Centre)

Bremerton Reserve Fleet piers packed with redundant Cold War naval power in 1997. The NEW JERSEY is at far left. Seven Knox-class frigates are sandwiched between her and the MIDWAY. Across the pier is the MISSOURI and at far right is the RANGER. The 46 Knox's were decommissioned between 1991 and 1994. Some were to be retained in reserve, but ultimately all were discarded. Some were scrapped, others sold overseas to Greece, Turkey and Taiwan. (Don Shelton)

Nuclear graveyard at the Puget Sound Naval Shipyard in 1997. The ships, stripped down to the upperdeck, are the remains of the cruisers VIRGINIA, TEXAS and the world's first nuclear-powered surface warship, LONG BEACH. The VIRGINIA and TEXAS were relatively young when they were stricken to avoid the cost of refueling them. All nuclear-powered naval vessels are dismantled at Puget Sound. The reactors are removed from the ships and taken to Hanford, Washington for burial. (Don Shelton)

From the 1960's to the 1980's the three missile submarines on the right, VON STEUBEN, ANDREW JACKSON, and NATHANAEL GREENE, were among those that conducted countless patrols in the ocean's depth, ready at any time to retaliate to a nuclear strike. Their place in the fleet, in 2002, had been taken by the huge Ohio class subs and this trio will be scrapped. In compliance with the Strategic Arms Limitation Talks (SALT) Treaty, their missile compartments have already been removed and the forward and aft sections welded together resulting in these stubby hulks. (Don Shelton)

This is Mooring Alpha at Puget Sound, nuclear cruisers and submarines waiting their turn to be scrapped. The cruisers are VIRGINIA (left), TEXAS, and LONG BEACH, all stripped to the main deck level. The stern of the TEXAS has been removed so she can fit into drydock with another sub. Just outboard of the LONG BEACH are the attack submarines CINCINNATI and OMAHA, both decommissioned after less than twenty years service. (Don Shelton)

A quartet of nuclear submarines is reduced to shards of scrap metal in Dry Dock 4, Puget Sound Naval Shipyard, in 1997. (Don Shelton)

Throughout the post war years and into the late 1950's, the back basin of the Philadelphia Navy Yard was lined with cruisers. Four decades later it is still used to store the discarded cruisers and destroyers of another age (upper right). Out in the Delaware River on 30 October 1995 are the battleships IOWA and WISCONSIN, the discarded carriers FORRESTAL and SARATOGA, the helicopter carriers IWO JIMA and GUADALCANAL. (Defense Visual Information Centre)

The last of their breed are the battleships WISCONSIN and IOWA on the Delaware River at the Philadelphia Naval Shipyard in 1995. All four Iowa's were struck from the Navy list that year. WISCONSIN and NEW JERSEY were reinstated a few years later, then IOWA was substituted for NEW JERSEY. IOWA was towed to San Francisco Bay in 2001, while the WISCONSIN was opened to the public at Norfolk, Virginia, in April 2001. (Defense Visual Information Centre)

The heavy cruiser DES MOINES, the "Daisy Mae", at Philadelphia. She shows the effects of her 30 years in the reserve fleet. She was stricken in 1991 along with the SALEM, but efforts to preserve her still continue in 2002. (William Blythe)

In the early 1990's the Belknap and Leahy classes of missile cruiser were taken out of service. None went into mothballs, all were stricken from the Naval Vessel Register. Here are two of them, the BIDDLE (left) and WAINWRIGHT, moored at the Philadelphia Naval Shipyard's back basin, where US Navy cruisers have been stored since 1946. (Brent Lundgren)

The MORTON, and another Forrest Sherman-class "tin can", swing gently at anchor at their Pearl Harbour moorings in October 1991. MORTON still wears her hull number, but that will soon be painted out and she will disappear into obscurity.
(Defense Visual Information Centre)

This is Middle Loch, Pearl Harbour, where the Charles F. Adams class destroyers HOEL, JOSEPH STRAUSS, HENRY B. WILSON and COCHRANE lie between the buoys after being paid off. The STRAUSS was later transferred to the Royal Hellenic Navy in 1991.
(Defense Visual Information Centre)

Moored among the destroyers and frigates in Pearl Harbour's Middle Loch, in May 2000, is the amphibious ship VANCOUVER. She served nearly three decades, not at all unusual in the US Navy with its excellent drydock and maintenance facilities.
(Christopher Vallery)

Nestled among the bigger guided-missile destroyers on 5 October 1993 at James River is the WILLIAM C. LAWE (4th from the right). She was a Gearing-class destroyer commissioned in 1946. She was sunk as a target in 1999, hundreds of miles east of Puerto Rico.
(Defense Visual Information Centre)

Not a fleet in port, but a fleet waiting to die. The Baltimore Salvage Company would soon start work on the destroyers in the foreground, while Seawitch Marine Salvage has already begun dismantling the carrier CORAL SEA (upper right) in this August 1994 photo of the Baltimore Fairfield Terminal.
(Defense Visual Information Centre)

A closer view of the destroyers berthed near the CORAL SEA shows what kind of shape they are in. Note the absence of hull numbers. In the foreground is the BLANDY, outboard of the FORREST SHERMAN. Behind, from front to back are the CLAUDE V. RICKETTS, the LAWRENCE and the BIGALOW. (Defense Visual Information Centre)

In drydock at the old Hunter's Point (San Francisco) Naval Shipyard, the frigate MEYERKORD is prepared for scrapping in May 2001. The ship is first stripped of anything useful; safes, telephones, evaporators and the like, before the breakers get to work. (Barbara Hilsz)

The scrapmen have been hard at work on the MEYERKORD's sister ship GRAY, in the same drydock. Not much is left of her, everything above the first platform deck is gone. To the left is the helicopter pad of the frigate LANG, also being scrapped. (Barbara Hilsz)

Most of these ships in this row of the James River Reserve Fleet are oilers, those vital auxiliary ships that extended the legs of the US Navy to any part of the globe even in the pre-nuclear days. The two big ships at the end, in this January 1996 photo, are the Henry J. Kaiser class fleet oilers BENJAMIN ISHERWOOD and the HENRY ECKFORD. Because of difficulties during their construction, they were laid up incomplete at the James River National Defense Reserve Fleet anchorage. (Defense Visual Information Centre)

Suisun Bay from the air. A couple of helicopter carriers, including the OKINAWA, on the left, and missile cruisers to the right.
(Leo Marriott)

Nine years after being stricken from the Naval Vessel Register, the destroyer COCHRANE was towed from her berth at Pearl Harbour to International Shipbreaking in Brownsville, Texas. As is the case with many an old vessel about to be broken up, former members of her crew paid her a last visit in March 2001 to shoot a few pictures and to say goodbye. (Don Reed)

HOWARD GILMORE was an American submarine captain and hero, and this tender was commissioned in his honour in 1944. She was stricken in 1980 but was retained for spare parts. This photograph was taken 8 October 1994 at Portsmouth, Virginia.
(Defense Visual Information Centre)

After 22 years in commission through four tours of duty and three wars, and 26 years in the reserve fleet, the NEW JERSEY completes her tow from Bremerton to Philadelphia on Veterans Day, 11 November 1999. Her days as a warship are over. She is now (2002) a museum in her home state, the sixth American battleship so preserved. (David Wells)

The SALEM was one of a trio of heavy cruisers completed after World War 2 with new rapid-firing eight inch guns. She served a decade with the fleet, then spent the next 32 years in reserve. Here, she comes home to Quincy, Massachusetts in 1994 where she joins the growing list of museum ships at ports throughout the United States. The SALEM played the role of the German pocket battleship GRAF SPEE in the film of "The Battle of the River Plate" (Andrew Toppan)

The world's first atomic warship, and the first submarine to operate under the North Pole, was the NAUTILUS. She is seen here being towed through the Panama Canal on 21 june 1985, on her way to Groton, Connecticut, where she was put on display at the Submarine force Museum on 11 April 1986.
(Defense Visual Information Centre)

The Korean War and the sad state of the navy's mine countermeasure forces was the impetus behind the construction of a large number of minesweepers in the early 1950's. One of the last of them, the ILLUSIVE, meets her end, in 1993, at Baltimore's Seawitch Salvage Company, just across the pier from the CORAL SEA. (Defense Visual Information Centre)

The partially scrapped missile cruiser HARRY E. YARNELL is seen outboard of the heavy cruiser DES MOINES in this view taken from the bridge of the BIDDLE, in the reserve basin of the Philadelphia Naval Shipyard in 1999. (Brent Lundgren)

The light carrier CABOT waits for the scrappers to begin their work on her in Brownsville, Texas, in 2000. Sadly, all efforts to preserve the CABOT, last of the light carriers and still configured much as she was in World War 2, had failed. (Iron Woman Foundation)

Painted on her starboard quarter are the two names she carried throughout her long career: CABOT in the United States Navy, and DEDALO in the Spanish Navy. Note the round, cruiser stern and the gun mount sponson, upon which sits a 40mm mount.
(Iron Woman Foundation)

Scrapping the diesel-electric submarine BARBEL, seen here on 4 JULY 1999, presented none of the complications of a nuclear-powered boat. She would soon be towed to a drydock to complete the job, without the worry of removing and transporting a reactor.
(William Michael Young)

She doesn't have the sleek lines of a battleship, or the imposing bulk of an aircraft carrier, but the repair ship JASON was an equally vital part of the fleet for the fifty one years she served. Falling scrap metal prices had saved her from the breakers when this shot was taken at Richmond in 1999. (Larry Drees)

The vessel on the left, in this 1997 photo, is the amphibious cargo ship TULARE. She commissioned in 1956 and spent the next 30 years carrying marines and their cargo around the Pacific. She paid off in 1986, was stricken from the reserve fleet in 1992, and was towed out to the Suisun Bay Reserve Fleet. The ship next to her is the Maritime Administration's NORTHERN LIGHT.

(William Michael Young)

Most of the upper works of the cruiser NEWPORT NEWS are gone in this view of her scrapping taken at a yard in New Orleans in 1993. She was a veteran of the Vietnam War, and was the United States Navy's last active heavy cruiser, decommissioning on 27 June 1975. She was stricken three years later and was sold to Southern Scrap Metals, arriving at New Orleans in March 1993. Scrapping was virtually complete by Autumn 1994. (Christopher Vallery)

The minelayer OGLALA was one of the victims of the Japanese attack on Pearl Harbour. Her hull was ruptured by the blast of a torpedo striking a cruiser alongside and she rolled over and sank in the shallow water. The subject of an intense salvage effort for nearly seven months, it wasn't until July 1942 that the OGLALA was finally drydocked for repairs. She was converted to a repair ship for internal combustion engines and decommissioned in 1946. Here she meets her end in December 1965 at the Joffe Brothers scrapyard in Richmond. (Naval Historical Centre)

At piers once lined with carefully preserved submarines and destroyer escorts, only a few nearly forgotten ships remain, saved only for use as targets. These are the World War 2 Fletcher-class destroyers PICKING and STODDARD. Both were decommissioned at Mare Island in 1969, and were still there in 1996 when this photograph was taken. By the following year they had been sunk as targets.
(Daniel Madsen)